The  Cookbook

Discover 30+ Different and Delicious Ways to Cook with Lavender!

BY: Allie Allen

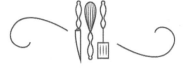

Copyright 2019 Allie Allen

Copyright Notes

This book is written as an informational tool. While the author has taken every precaution to ensure the accuracy of the information provided therein, the reader is warned that they assume all risk when following the content. The author will not be held responsible for any damages that may occur as a result of the readers' actions.

The author does not give permission to reproduce this book in any form, including but not limited to: print, social media posts, electronic copies or photocopies, unless permission is expressly given in writing.

Table of Contents

Introduction 6

1. Orange Lavender Mimosa 7

2. Pineapple Lavender Smoothie 9

3. Lavender Infused Lemonade 11

4. Lavender Lemon Sorbet 13

5. Lavender and Lemon Tart 15

6. Lavender and Lemon Bars 19

7. Lavender and Olive Oil Madeleines 22

8. Strawberry and Lavender Chiller 25

9. Mint Lavender Lemonade 27

10. Fresh Orange and Lavender Cupcakes 29

11. White Chocolate and Lavender Mousse 33

12. Lemon and Lavender Ice Cream 36

13. Orange Lavender Tart 38

14. Buttermilk Lavender Ice Cream 42

15. Lavender Chiller 45

16. Lemon Lavender Mimosa 47

17. Smoked Duck and Grilled Plum Salad 49

18. Berry Lavender Sorbet 51

19. Pineapple Lavender Mimosa 53

20. Blueberry Lavender Compote 55

21. Vanilla White Chocolate Lavender Macarons 57

22. Lemon and Lavender Cupcakes 60

23. Slow Roasted Root Vegetables 64

24. Duck Breasts with Orange-Lavender Sauce 66

25. Chocolate Lavender Fudge 70

26. Lavender Green Tea 72

27. Dutch Oven Lavender Bread 74

28. Lavender Almond Fudge 77

29. Dark Chocolate Lavender Tart 79

30. Lavender Cream 82

Conclusion 84

About the Author 85

Author's Afterthoughts 87

Introduction

Looking for ways to use lavender in recipes? If you answered yes, then this recipe book is for you! Filled with 30 different and delicious recipes, this book has everything you need to put up delicious recipes that are filled with just the right amount of lavender for you to experience its herbal undertones.

From lavender lemonade to lavender roasted veggies, this book has something for everyone and every occasion. So, what are you waiting for? Load up on lavender and let's begin!

1. Orange Lavender Mimosa

Orange mimosa infused with a delicious lavender syrup.

Makes: 8 servings

Prep: 5 mins

Cook: -

Ingredients:

- 1 ounce lavender syrup
- 8 ounces orange juice
- 8 ounces champagne

Directions:

Puree all the ingredients in a blender and serve with orange slices!

2. Pineapple Lavender Smoothie

A refreshing, fruity and floral pineapple and lavender smoothie recipe.

Makes: 2 servings

Prep: 5 mins

Cook: -

Ingredients:

- ¼ ounce lavender syrup
- 2 cups coconut water
- 1 cup pineapple chunks
- 1/3 cup quinoa flakes
- 1/2 cup pasteurized egg whites
- 1/4 cup unsalted raw or roasted almonds
- 1 tsp. vanilla extract or 1/2 tsp. almond extract
- 1/4 tsp. ground cloves
- 1 cup frozen blueberries

Directions:

Blend all the ingredients until smooth, about 30 seconds.

Divide between two glasses and serve.

3. Lavender Infused Lemonade

A refreshing and delicious lavender lemonade recipe.

Makes: 12 servings

Prep: 10 mins

Cook: -

Ingredients:

- 2 ½ tbsp. dried lavender
- 4 cups cold water
- 3 lemons, washed and deseeded
- Juice of 1 large lemon
- ¾ cup sugar

Directions:

Bring five cups of water to boil. Add in the lavender and let steep for about an hour. Strain the infused water and put in a blender.

Add all the remaining ingredients on high speed in the blender. Strain again before serving.

4. Lavender Lemon Sorbet

Tangy and refreshing, this lemon sorbet is refreshing, hydrating, and perfect for summer.

Makes: 6 servings

Prep: 1 hr.

Cook: -

Ingredients:

- 2 cups water
- 1 cup sugar
- ½ tsp lavender, ground
- 1 1/2 cups lemon juice
- 1 tablespoon lemon zest

Directions:

Mix together all the ingredients in your bowl, then pour it in the container of your ice cream maker.

Freeze according to manufacturer's instructions, then store in an airtight container in your freezer.

5. Lavender and Lemon Tart

Sweet, zesty and light, this tart is the perfect after-dessert treat.

Makes: 8 servings

Prep: 2 hrs. 10 mins

Cook: 30 mins

Ingredients:

For the pastry:

- 1 ¾ cup of all-purpose flour
- ¼ cup icing sugar
- ½ tsp of salt
- ¼ cup of unsweetened cocoa powder
- ½ cup of unsalted butter
- 1 egg yolk
- 2 ½ tbsp. cold water

For the tart:

- ½ cup dark, grated finely
- 2 large lemons
- 1 tsp dried lavender
- 2/3 cup of caster sugar
- 4 eggs
- ½ cup + 2 tbsp. heavy cream
- Icing sugar, for dusting

Directions:

For the pastry:

In a bowl, mix together the salt, cocoa, sugar, and flour. Add the butter and mix. Add the egg yolk and then the water. Mix well. Fold into a lump. Wrap with cling film and chill for 40 minutes.

Roll out the pastry evenly onto the base of a well-greased 9-inch spring form cake tin and chill for 90 minutes.

For the tart:

Preheat oven to 400°F. Place in the oven for 15 minutes. Do not overbake. Immediately sprinkle the hot pastry evenly with the grated chocolate. Set aside. Reduce oven temperature to 325°F.

Grate the lemon zest into a large bowl. Add the lavender and sugar and the juice from the lemons. Mix well. Whisk in the eggs and then the cream until well incorporated. Pour over the pastry in the spring form tin and bake for about 30 minutes or until set.

Release the spring form-tin sides to aid cooling. Allow to cool completely. Dust with sugar and serve.

6. Lavender and Lemon Bars

Delicious and delicate lavender and lemon bars that taste like a dream.

Makes: 32 servings

Prep: 10 mins

Cook: 25 mins

Ingredients:

For the crust:

- 1 ½ cups unsalted butter, cold, cut into cubes
- ¾ cup white sugar
- 3 cups all-purpose flour

For the filling:

- 3 cups white sugar
- ½ cup all-purpose flour
- 8 eggs
- 1 tsp dried lavender
- 1 ½ cup lemon juice
- 2 tbsp. lemon zest

Directions:

Preheat oven to 350°F.

For the pastry:

Combine the sugar, flour, and unsalted butter in a food processor and process for 1 minute or until a ball is formed.

Press dough into a 16x16 inch pre-greased baking pan and bake for 25-30 minutes or until golden-brown.

In a large bowl, whisk the sugar, flour, lavender, eggs, juice and zest. Set aside for 20 minutes while the crust bakes.

When the crust is done, whisk the mixture again and then pour it onto the crust. Place in the oven for another 25 minutes or until set.

Serve.

7. Lavender and Olive Oil Madeleines

Light, soft and scrumptious lavender and olive oil madeleines recipe.

Makes: 1 dozen

Prep: 15 mins

Cook: 15 mins

Ingredients:

- 2 eggs
- ¼ cup brown sugar
- ¼ cup extra-virgin olive oil
- 1 ½ tbsp. freshly squeezed lemon juice
- ½ tsp vanilla extract
- 1/8 tsp salt
- 1 tsp lavender, ground
- 1 tsp baking powder
- ½ cup + 1 tbsp. all-purpose flour
- Zest of ½ a lemon

Directions:

Preheat oven to 350°F. Lightly grease a madeleine pan.

Beat the eggs using an electric mixer. Add in the sugar and beat for 2 minutes. Next, add in the olive oil, lavender and juice and beat again before adding in the remaining ingredients. Beat until just combined. Cover and refrigerate mixture for 10 minutes.

Remove and stir once before spooning mixture into the pan. Bake for 10-15 minutes or until done.

Cool before serving.

8. Strawberry and Lavender Chiller

Sweet, fresh and delicious strawberry and lavender chiller.

Makes: 12 servings

Prep: 10 mins

Cook: -

Ingredients:

- 4 cups cold water
- 3 lemons, washed and deseeded
- ¼ oz lavender syrup
- ¾ cup of sugar
- 2 cups strawberries, fresh or frozen

Directions:

Blend all of your ingredients on high speed in a high-quality blender. Strain before serving.

9. Mint Lavender Lemonade

Minty and refreshing lemonade drink.

Makes: 12 servings

Prep: 10 mins

Cook: -

Ingredients:

- 4 cups cold water
- 3 lemons, washed and deseeded
- Juice of 1 large lemon
- ¾ cup sugar
- 1 oz lavender syrup
- ½ cup mint leaves

Directions:

Blend all ingredients except mint leaves on high speed in a high-quality blender. Strain and then add in the mint leaves. Let it sit for 1 hr. before serving.

10. Fresh Orange and Lavender Cupcakes

Delicious and fresh orange and lavender cupcakes. A favorite with tea—both hot and iced.

Makes: 16 cupcakes

Prep: 30 minutes

Cook: 15 to 18 minutes

Ingredients:

For the orange cupcakes:

- 1 package (15 ounces) yellow cake mix
- ¼ cup granulated sugar
- ⅔ cup fresh orange juice
- ½ cup vegetable oil
- 3 large eggs
- 1 tsp lavender
- 1 teaspoon vanilla extract
- 1 teaspoon grated orange zest

For the orange cream cheese frosting:

- 4 ounces dairy-free cream cheese, softened
- 4 tablespoons margarine, at room temperature
- 3 cups confectioners' sugar
- 2 teaspoons grated fresh orange zest

Directions:

Cupcakes: Preheat the oven to 350°F. Line 16 cupcake cups with paper liners.

Place the cake mix, granulated sugar, orange juice, oil, eggs, lavender, vanilla, and orange zest in a mixing bowl and beat with an electric mixer on low until the ingredients are just combined, about 30 seconds. Increase speed to med & beat the batter until it is smooth, 1 to 1½ minutes. Scoop ¼ cup batter into each of the lined cupcake cups and place the pans in the oven side by side.

Bake the cupcakes for15 to 18 mins. Transfer your pans to wire racks and let the cupcakes cool in the pans for 1 to 2 minutes, then carefully transfer the cupcakes to the racks to cool completely before frosting, about 30 minutes longer.

Meanwhile make the dairy-free orange cream cheese frosting:

Place your cream cheese and margarine in a mixing bowl and quietly beat with a mixer on low speed until creamy, about 30 seconds. Stop & add the sugar and orange zest a little bit at a time, beating on low speed for about 30 seconds. Increase the mixer speed to med & beat for1 to 2 minutes longer.

Frost the cupcakes generously with the frosting. As the frosting is soft, place the cupcakes in a cake saver and refrigerate them if not serving them in the next 4 hours.

11. White Chocolate and Lavender Mousse

This whipped and creamy white chocolate mousse recipe is an elegant, easy and absolutely delicious recipe.

Makes: 8 servings

Prep: 5 mins

Cook: 10 mins plus cooling time

Ingredients:

- 4 egg yolks
- 4 tbsp. white sugar
- 2 ½ cups heavy whipping cream, divided
- 1 cup white chocolate chips
- ½ tsp ground lavender
- Chocolate shavings, to serve

Directions:

In a bowl, beat the eggs together on high speed for about 4 minutes or until thick. Stream in the sugar and beat for about a minute more or until combined.

In a large saucepan, heat 1 cup heavy whipping cream until hot but not boiling. Carefully add in half of the cream to the egg mixture and stir until combined. Add the mixture back to the remaining cream in the saucepan and cook on low for about 4 minutes, stirring constantly, until thickened.

Add in the white chocolate chips and lavender and stir until well combined. Cover & place in the refrigerator for about 2 hours, stirring every half hour.

In a medium bowl, beat the remaining heavy whipping cream using a hand mixer on high speed for about 4 minutes or until stiff. Gently fold in the white chocolate mixture. Divide between glasses and top with chocolate shavings.

Serve.

12. Lemon and Lavender Ice Cream

This lemon and lavender infused ice cream is the perfect treat for the hot summer months.

Makes: 6 servings

Prep: 3 hrs.

Cook: 10 mins

Ingredients:

- 3 cups milk
- 2 tsp. lemon extract
- 3 tsp. lemon juice
- 2 tsp. lemon zest
- ½ tsp ground lavender
- Lemonade 1/3 cup
- 2/3 cup white sugar
- 6 egg yolks

Directions:

Beat the yolks and sugar for about 4 minutes or until lightened in both color and surface.

In a saucepan, bring the 3 cups of milk to a boil. Lower the heat and then add in the sugar mixture, whisking constantly until thickened. Add in the zest, extract, lavender, and juice and whisk until well combined. Set aside to cool and then place in the fridge for 3 hours.

Churn in an ice cream maker.

13. Orange Lavender Tart

Sweet, zesty and light, this is a delicious orange and lavender tart recipe.

Makes: 8 servings

Prep: 2 hrs. 10 mins

Cook: 30 mins

Ingredients:

For the pastry:

- 1 ¾ cup all-purpose flour
- 4 tbsp. icing sugar
- ½ tsp salt
- ¼ cup unsweetened cocoa powder
- ½ cup unsalted butter
- 1 egg yolk
- 2 ½ tbsp. cold water

For the tart:

- ½ cup dark chocolate, grated finely
- 2 oranges
- 1 tsp dried lavender
- 2/3 cup caster sugar
- 4 eggs
- ½ cup + 2 tbsp. heavy cream
- Icing sugar, for dusting

Directions:

For the pastry:

In a bowl, combine together the salt, cocoa, sugar, and flour. Add the butter and mix. Add the egg yolk and then the water. Mix well. Fold into a lump. Wrap with cling film and chill for 40 minutes.

Roll out the pastry evenly onto the base of a well-greased 9-inch spring form cake tin and chill for 90 minutes.

For the tart:

Preheat oven to 400°F. Place in the oven for 15 minutes. Do not overbake. Immediately sprinkle the hot pastry evenly with the grated chocolate. Set aside. Reduce oven temperature to 325°F.

Grate the zest into a bowl. Add the sugar, lavender and the juice from the oranges. Mix well. Whisk in the eggs and then the cream until well incorporated. Pour over the pastry in the spring form tin and bake for about 30 minutes or until set.

Release the spring form-tin sides to aid cooling. Allow to cool completely. Dust with sugar and serve.

14. Buttermilk Lavender Ice Cream

Enriched with just a little double cream, this unusual ice cream tastes far more luxurious than it really is.

Makes: 6 servings

Prep: 3 hrs. 10 mins

Cook: 5 mins

Ingredients:

- 1 cup buttermilk
- 4 tbsp. heavy cream
- 1 tbsp dried lavender
- 2 eggs
- 2 tbsp. clear honey
- Fresh fruit purée, to serve

Directions:

Place the buttermilk and cream in a pan with lavender, and heat gently over 2 low heat until the mixture is almost boiling. Let it steep for 20 mins then strain and heat until warm.

Place the eggs in a bowl over a pan of hot water and whisk until they are pale and thick. Add the heated buttermilk in a thin stream, while whisking hard. Continue whisking over the hot water until the mixture has thickened slightly.

Whisk in the honey and vanilla essence, if using. Spoon the mixture into a freezer-proof container and freeze until firm.

Spoon the firm ice cream onto a sheet of non-stick baking paper. Roll it up in the paper to form a cylinder and freeze again until firm. Serve the ice cream on plates in slices.

15. Lavender Chiller

Sweet, fresh and delicious lavender chiller.

Makes: 12 servings

Prep: 10 mins

Cook: -

Ingredients:

- 4 cups cold water
- 3 lemons, washed and deseeded
- ¼ oz lavender syrup
- ¾ cup sugar

Directions:

Blend all of your ingredients on high speed in a high-quality blender. Strain before serving.

16. Lemon Lavender Mimosa

Lemon mimosa infused with a delicious lavender syrup.

Makes: 8 servings

Prep: 5 mins

Cook: -

Ingredients:

- 1 ounce lavender syrup
- 8 ounces lemon juice
- 8 ounces champagne

Directions:

Puree all the ingredients in a blender and serve with orange slices!

17. Smoked Duck and Grilled Plum Salad

A light and delicious salad with smoked duck, watercress, grilled plums and lavender.

Makes: 8 servings

Prep: 15 mins

Cook: 10 mins

Ingredients:

- 6 tbsp. extra virgin olive oil
- 2 tbsp. vinegar
- ½ tsp fresh lavender
- 8 plums
- 5 cups watercress
- 1 cup smoked duck

Directions:

In a bowl, combine together the olive oil, lavender, vinegar, some salt and pepper.

Cut the plums into quarters and grill for 2-3 mins on each side until charred and a bit caramelized. Toss the watercress with the dressing, & then divide between plates. Top with the plums and smoked duck.

Serve.

18. Berry Lavender Sorbet

Berries work great together as their taste complement each other. This sorbet is rich and creamy and simply delicious in a hot summer day.

Makes: 6 servings

Prep: 30 mins

Cook: -

Ingredients:

- 1 cup strawberry
- 1 cup blackberry
- 1/2 cup sugar
- ½ tsp lavender leaves
- 1 teaspoon lemon juice

Directions:

Put all ingredients in a processor and puree. Using an ice-cream maker, churn the mixture and freeze according to manufacturer's instructions.

Serve.

19. Pineapple Lavender Mimosa

Pineapple mimosa infused with a delicious lavender syrup.

Makes: 8 servings

Prep: 5 mins

Cook: -

Ingredients:

- 1 ounce lavender syrup
- 8 ounces pineapple juice
- 8 ounces champagne

Directions:

Puree all the ingredients in a blender and serve with orange slices!

20. Blueberry Lavender Compote

Use this fruit compote instead of maple syrup on pancakes and waffles or try stirring it into yogurt.

Makes: 6 servings

Prep: 5 mins

Cook: 5 mins

Ingredients:

- 2 cups (480 ml) frozen or fresh blueberries
- 1 Tbsp (15 ml) lemon juice
- 1 Tbsp (15 ml) brown-rice syrup, yacon syrup, honey or Sucanat
- 1 tsp (5 ml) arrowroot starch
- 2 fresh lavender sprigs
- Pinch sea salt

Directions:

Combine all of ingredients in a saucepan & bring to a simmer on medium-high heat, stirring occasionally. Reduce heat to gently simmer and cook until slightly thickened, and some blueberries have broken down, 2 or 3 minutes. Remove from heat and let cool slightly and then remove the lavender sprigs.

Refrigerate any unused compote.

21. Vanilla White Chocolate Lavender Macarons

Classic macarons with a white chocolate, lavender and vanilla filling.

Makes: 48 macarons

Prep: 35 mins

Cook: 12 mins

Ingredients:

Shells:

- 2 egg whites
- 5 tbsp. superfine sugar
- 2/3 cup + 8 tsp icing sugar
- 2/3 cup almond flour

Filling:

- ½ cup white chocolate, chopped
- 8 tsp heavy cream
- 1 tsp ground lavender
- ½ tsp vanilla extract

Directions:

Preheat the oven to 320°F. Line a pan with baking paper and set aside.

Combine the superfine sugar, almond flour and color in a bowl.

In a separate bowl, beat the egg whites with a mixer until foamy. Add in ½ the sugar mixture and beat until soft peaks form. Add in the other ½ and beat until stiff peaks form. Fold in the icing sugar. Put mixture into a large piping bag and pipe dollops onto the pan. Gently tap the pan to let out any air bubbles. Let it sit for ½ an hour.

Place in the oven and bake for 10-12 minutes.

Filling:

Heat the cream in a bowl until almost boiling. Add in the chocolate, lavender and vanilla & let it sit for 2 minutes. Stir. Refrigerate to thicken slightly and then proceed to piping the macarons.

Serve.

22. Lemon and Lavender Cupcakes

Delicious and fresh lemon and lavender cupcakes with a lemon cream cheese frosting.

Makes: 16 cupcakes

Prep: 30 minutes

Cook: 15 to 18 minutes

Ingredients:

For the lemon lavender cupcakes:

- 1 package (15 ounces) yellow cake mix
- ¼ cup granulated sugar
- ⅔ cup fresh lemon juice
- ½ cup vegetable oil
- 3 large eggs
- 1 tsp lavender
- 1 teaspoon vanilla extract
- 1 teaspoon grated lemon zest

For the lemon cream cheese frosting:

- 4 ounces cream cheese, softened
- 4 tablespoons margarine, at room temperature
- 3 cups confectioners' sugar
- 2 teaspoons grated fresh lemon zest

Directions:

Cupcakes: Preheat the oven to 350°F. Line 16 cupcake cups with paper liners.

Place the cake mix, granulated sugar, juice, oil, eggs, lavender, vanilla, and zest in a mixing bowl and beat with an electric mixer on low until the ingredients are just combined, about 30 seconds. Increase speed to med & beat the batter until it is smooth, 1 to 1½ minutes. Scoop ¼ cup batter into each of the lined cupcake cups and place the pans in the oven side by side.

Bake the cupcakes for15 to 18 mins. Transfer the pans to wire racks and let the cupcakes cool in the pans for 1 to 2 minutes, then carefully transfer the cupcakes to the racks to cool completely before frosting, about 30 minutes longer.

Meanwhile make the lemon cream cheese frosting:

Place the cream cheese and margarine in a mixing bowl and beat with a mixer on low speed until creamy, about 30 seconds. Stop & add the sugar and zest a little bit at a time, beating on low speed for about 30 seconds. Increase the mixer speed to med & beat for1 to 2 minutes longer.

Frost the cupcakes generously with the frosting. As the frosting is soft, place the cupcakes in a cake saver and refrigerate them if not serving them in the next 4 hours.

23. Slow Roasted Root Vegetables

Delicious root veggies with garlic and lavender.

Makes: 6 servings

Prep: 10 mins

Cook: 75-90 mins

Ingredients:

- 1 bag baby carrots
- 2 onions, peeled and cut in wedges
- 3 parsnips, peeled and cut into thick slices
- 1 lb. baby red potatoes, washed
- 6 cloves whole garlic, peeled
- 3 Tbs. olive oil
- ½ tsp. sea salt
- ½ tsp. ground black pepper
- 1 tbsp. dried lavender

Directions:

In a 12" cast iron Dutch oven with feet, combine vegetables and garlic cloves. Drizzle with olive oil and mix to coat evenly. Add salt, pepper and lavender. Gently mix together.

Arrange 4 hot coals in a circle and place Dutch oven over coals. Cover with flat lid and top with 6 more hot coals. Let roast for 75-90 minutes, adding fresh coals as needed.

Serve hot.

24. Duck Breasts with Orange-Lavender Sauce

Leaving the skin on the duck breast gives the duck its wonderful flavor, along with a delicious, crispy skin.

Makes: 4 servings

Prep: 10 mins

Cook: 20 mins

Ingredients:

SPICE RUB

- 2 teaspoons kosher salt or fleur de sel
- 1 tablespoon packed light brown sugar
- 2 teaspoons fennel seed
- 1 tablespoon fresh rosemary
- 2 teaspoons dried lavender
- 2 teaspoons coriander seed, or 1 teaspoon ground coriander
- ¼ teaspoon ground ginger
- 1 teaspoon fresh oregano
- 2 large sage leaves
- 1 teaspoon fresh thyme leaves
- ½ teaspoon grated lemon zest
- 4 boneless, skin-on duck breasts (about 2 pounds total), at room temperature

ORANGE-LAVENDER SAUCE

- ¼ cup vinegar
- 2 tablespoons orange juice
- 1 cup low-sodium chicken stock
- 2 teaspoons honey
- 1 teaspoon coarsely chopped lavender leaves
- 1 tablespoon unsalted butter

Directions:

To prepare the rub, combine the salt, brown sugar, fennel seed, lavender, rosemary, coriander seed, ginger, oregano, sage, thyme, and lemon zest in a coffee or spice grinder and grind until smooth.

Preheat to 425°F.

To prepare the duck, rinse the breasts and pat dry. Remove any extra skin from the meat side of the breasts, leaving a ¼-inch overhang on the edges. Score the skin in a crosshatch pattern, making 6 to 8 cuts, ½ inch deep, in one direction and another 6 to 8 cuts in the other direction. Try not to cut through the meat. Coat duck with the spice rub mixture.

Heat iron skillet over medium-high heat for 3 minutes. Add the duck breasts & sear for 5 minutes. The skin should be crisp and golden brown.

Reduce the heat to med-low, turn the breasts over and cook for 2 minutes, and then place the skillet in the oven. Roast until the duck is cooked to your liking. Transfer to a plate & cover with foil.

To prepare the sauce, discard all but 2 tablespoons fat from the skillet, and place the skillet over medium-high heat. Add the vinegar, and orange juice, scraping up the browned bits and stirring them into the sauce. Boil until slightly reduced. Add the chicken stock, honey, and lavender and bring to a gentle boil until slightly reduced again, about 2 minutes. Reduce heat & whisk in the butter.

Slice the duck breasts ¼ inch thick at a 45° angle. Serve and spoon about 3 tbsp of sauce over each serving.

25. Chocolate Lavender Fudge

A delicious chocolate fudge recipe that's super creamy and unusual!

Makes: 18 servings

Prep: 10 mins plus chilling time

Cook: 2 mins

Ingredients:

- 1 ¼ cup dark or milk chocolate chips
- 7 oz. condensed milk
- 1 tbsp. unsalted butter
- ¼ cup + 3 tbsp. icing sugar
- 1 tbsp. ground lavender

Directions:

Line a 4x4 baking dish with baking paper and set aside.

In a large bowl, place the chocolate chips, condensed milk, lavender and butter and melt in a microwave in 20 second intervals until smooth. Add in the icing sugar and mix until well combined.

Press the mixture into the baking dish and smoothen out the top. Place in the refrigerator for about 1 hr. or until set.

Serve and enjoy!

26. Lavender Green Tea

Lavender tea with lemongrass and mint.

Makes: 8 servings

Prep: 5 mins plus steeping time

Cook: -

Ingredients:

- 8 cups water
- 1 sprig mint
- 3 green tea bags
- ½ tbsp. dried lemongrass
- ½ tbsp. dried lavender

Directions:

Put the water in a large jug. Add in the sprig of mint and tea bags. Put the dried lavender and lemongrass in a tea ball and put it in the water. Let it steep for 2 hrs and then serve.

27. Dutch Oven Lavender Bread

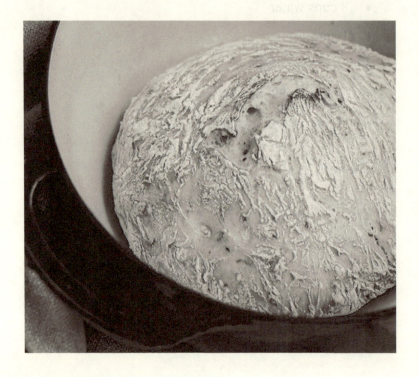

A delicious herbed bread recipe.

Makes: 4-6 servings

Prep: 15 mins

Inactive Time: 12 hrs

Cook: 45 mins

Ingredients:

- 2 tbsp. olive oil, plus more for the bowl
- 4 cups all-purpose flour
- 2 teaspoons sea salt
- 1 tbsp fresh lavender
- 1 tbsp fresh oregano
- 1 teaspoon active dry yeast
- 2 cups warm water

Directions:

Grease a bowl with a bit olive oil & set aside.

In another large bowl, mix the flour, sea salt, herbs and yeast.

Pour the warm water over the flour mixture and stir well to incorporate. Transfer the dough to the oiled bowl, cover loosely with a clean kitchen towel, and let rise for 12 hours or overnight.

Preheat the oven to 450°F.

Put the Dutch oven in.

Transfer the dough to the warmed Dutch oven. Cover the pot and return it to the oven for 40 minutes.

Remove the lid & bake for 15 minutes, until browned on top and baked through.

Let cool before slicing and serving warm.

28. Lavender Almond Fudge

This fudge recipe is so intensely creamy, rich and not to mention easy, you'll want to spoil yourself with it as often as possible.

Makes: 18 servings

Prep: 5 mins plus chilling time

Cook: 10 mins

Ingredients:

- 1 16 oz. pack of milk chocolate
- 1 14-oz can of sweetened condensed milk
- 1 ½ cups of almonds, chopped
- 1 tbsp. ground lavender

Directions:

Cover an 8x8 inch baking pan with aluminum foil and grease lightly with cooking spray.

In a saucepan set over medium heat, add in the condensed milk. When the milk starts to simmer, add in the milk chocolate. Cook for 1 to 2 minutes or until melted and smooth.

Remove from heat and add in the ground lavender and 1 cup of chopped almonds. Stir until well combined.

Pour into the baking dish and top with the remaining chopped almonds.

Cover and refrigerate for at least 1 hour.

Slice and serve. Enjoy!

29. Dark Chocolate Lavender Tart

Lavender and dark chocolate tart with a chocolate shortbread pastry crust.

Makes: 4 servings

Prep: 20 mins

Cook: 20 mins

Ingredients:

For the chocolate shortbread pastry:

- 1 ¼ cups all-purpose flour
- 3/8 cup unsalted butter
- Generous 3/8 cup white sugar
- 2 egg yolks
- 1/4 tsp baking powder
- 7 tsp cocoa powder
- Vanilla powder
- Salt

For the filling:

- Generous 3/8 cup cream
- 2 tsp glucose syrup
- 8 oz. dark chocolate
- 2 tsp dried lavender

For the decoration:

- 9 oz. fresh blackberries
- Confectioners' (icing) sugar

Directions:

Prepare the shortbread pastry: Mix the softened butter with the sugar, stir in a pinch of salt and the egg. Add the flour, baking powder, cocoa and a pinch of vanilla powder, then knead briefly until you have a smooth, even paste.

Plastic wrap the dough and refrigerate for one hour. On a lightly floured surface, roll out 9 oz. of the shortbread pastry to a thickness of 1/8 in (3 mm).

Line a buttered, floured cake tin with the pastry. Spread with jam and bake at 350 °F (180 °C) for 18 to 20 minutes. Remove and cool, then remove the tart from the tin.

Chop the dark chocolate & put it in a bowl with the lavender. Boil the cream with the syrup and pour it over the chocolate and lavender. Mix well until you have smooth, velvety cream.

Leave to cool and pour into the tart shell until it is filled up to the brim. Garnish with fresh berries, which have been washed and dried. Sprinkle with confectioners' sugar before serving.

30. Lavender Cream

Use this cream to top cakes, cupcakes and even fruit.

Makes: 3 cups

Prep: 10 mins

Cook: 5 mins

Ingredients:

- 3 cups heavy cream
- 6 tbsp honey
- 1 tsp dried lavender

Directions:

Bring all 3 ingredients to a boil. Remove and let it steep for 30 mins. Strain and then cover and refrigerate until ready to serve.

Conclusion

Well there you have it! 30 of the most delicious and flavorful lavender recipes for you to try! Make sure to try out each and every one of them and don't forget to share with your friends and family!

About the Author

Allie Allen developed her passion for the culinary arts at the tender age of five when she would help her mother cook for their large family of 8. Even back then, her family knew this would be more than a hobby for the young Allie and when she graduated from high school, she applied to cooking school in London. It had always been a dream of the young chef to study with some of Europe's best and she made it happen by attending the Chef Academy of London.

After graduation, Allie decided to bring her skills back to North America and open up her own restaurant. After 10 successful years as head chef and owner, she decided to sell her business and pursue other career avenues. This monumental decision led Allie to her true calling, teaching. She also started to write e-books for her students to study at home for practice. She is now the proud author of several e-books and gives private and semi-private cooking lessons to a range of students at all levels of experience.

Stay tuned for more from this dynamic chef and teacher when she releases more informative e-books on cooking and baking in the near future. Her work is infused with stores and anecdotes you will love!

Author's Afterthoughts

I can't tell you how grateful I am that you decided to read my book. My most heartfelt thanks that you took time out of your life to choose my work and I hope you find benefit within these pages.

There are so many books available today that offer similar content so that makes it even more humbling that you decided to buying mine.

Tell me what you thought! I am eager to hear your opinion and ideas on what you read as are others who are looking for a good book to buy. Leave a review on Amazon.com so others can benefit from your wisdom!

With much thanks,

Allie Allen

Made in United States
Troutdale, OR
03/28/2024

18800163R00054